LANGUAGE ARTS EXPLORER

PROPERTIES
OF MATTER

by Rebecca Hirsch

SCIENCE LAB:
PROPERTIES OF MATTER

CHERRY LAKE PUBLISHING • ANN ARBOR, MICHIGAN

CHERRY LAKE
Publishing

Published in the United States of America
by Cherry Lake Publishing
Ann Arbor, Michigan
www.cherrylakepublishing.com

Printed in the United States of America
Corporate Graphics Inc
September 2011
CLFA09

Consultants: Heather Abushanab, adjunct professor, Wentworth Institute of Technology; Gail Saunders-Smith, associate professor of literacy, Beeghly College of Education, Youngstown State University

Editorial direction: Book design and illustration:
Lisa Owings   Kazuko Collins

Photo credits: Alexander Fediachov/iStockphoto, cover, 1; NASA, ESA, and M. Livio and the Hubble 20th Anniversary Team (STScl), 5; Karen Borozinski/Bigstock, 7; Sergey Dolgikh/ Shutterstock Images, 9; John Anderson/Bigstock, 11; Bigstock, 13; Shutterstock Images, 14; Leah-Anne Thompson/Bigstock, 17; Scott Griessel/Bigstock, 19; Darren J. Bradley/ Shutterstock Images, 21; Laurence Gough/Bigstock, 22; Fotolia, 25; Mike V. Shuman/ Shutterstock Images, 27

Library of Congress Cataloging-in-Publication Data
Hirsch, Rebecca E.
 Science lab. Properties of matter / by Rebecca Hirsch.
    p. cm. – (Language arts explorer. Science lab)
 ISBN 978-1-61080-206-2 – ISBN 978-1-61080-295-6 (pbk.)
 1. Matter–Juvenile literature. I. Title. II. Title: Properties of matter.
 QC173.16.H57 2011
 530.4–dc23
                                2011015131

Cherry Lake Publishing would like to acknowledge the work of The Partnership for 21st Century Skills. Please visit www.21stCenturySkills.org for more information.

TABLE OF CONTENTS

You are being given a mission. The facts in What You Know will help you accomplish it. Remember the clues from What You Know while you are reading the story. The clues and the story will help you answer the questions at the end of the book. Have fun on this adventure!

All things are made of matter. Your mission is to investigate the properties of matter. What are the different kinds of matter? Do all kinds of matter behave in the same ways? How do the properties of matter change? Why are scientists interested in studying these changes? Read the facts in What You Know, and then start your investigation into the world of matter.

WHAT YOU KNOW

★ Everything in the universe is made of matter, from the earth and moon to the sun and stars. Matter is anything you can touch: the rocks on the ground, the clothes you are wearing, and the book you are holding.

★ All matter takes up space. **Volume** is a measure of how much space matter uses.

★ Different types of matter are called materials. Different materials behave differently and are used for different jobs. Fabric is strong but flexible, which makes it good

In our own galaxy, this cloud of matter is forming new stars.

for clothing. Steel is hard and sturdy, which makes it good for buildings and cars.

Now you're ready to take part in a one-week investigation called "Matter Explorers." Read Ian Whitman's journal about attending a science camp.

Today was my first day of science camp. We will be working in a laboratory in teams. Right away, my team and I learned that everything in the universe is made of matter. Matter is all around me. My sneakers are made of matter, and so is the lab coat I am wearing. The chair I am sitting on is matter—even my hair and teeth and skin.

Our camp instructor, Dr. Ines Gonzalez, told us that matter takes up space. It is made of tiny particles called **molecules**. Water molecules are so tiny that there are millions in just one drop!

Next we learned about the different states, or kinds, of matter. Dr. Gonzalez pointed out the stations she had set up around the room.

At our first station, we found some rocks, blocks of wood, and a bag of coins. These are all solids. Dr. Gonzalez explained that a solid is something hard that holds its shape. "The molecules in a solid are close together and don't move around much. Solids aren't squeezable. You can't force a solid into a smaller space. Solids also don't flow. You can't pour a block of wood."

At the next station, we found bottles filled with water, molasses, and ketchup. "These are all liquids!" I announced.

"That's right," said Dr. Gonzalez. "The molecules in liquids are farther apart than in solids, and they move around a lot more. Unlike solids, liquids don't have their own shape. They take the shape of their container. When you pour a liquid from a round container into a square one, its shape changes." She also told us that all liquids flow, but not at the same speed.

Water molecules tend to stick together. How many drops of water can you fit on a penny?

We raced the liquids in the bottles by pouring them into cups. Water flowed the fastest, while molasses oozed the slowest. Dr. Gonzalez had us investigate what would happen if we squeezed the soft plastic molasses bottle. The molasses dribbled down the side. "Like solids," Dr. Gonzalez said, "liquids can't be **compressed**, which means they can't easily be forced into a smaller space."

At our last station, we investigated air. Air is a gas. We learned that gas molecules don't stay together. They bounce all over their containers. If you put a certain amount of gas in a bigger container, the molecules spread out to fill it. If you put the same amount of gas in a smaller container, the molecules get closer together. I raised my hand. "Dr. Gonzalez, if gases can shrink and expand, does that mean they can be compressed?"

She didn't give us an answer. Instead, she handed us a bag of balloons and told us to investigate. We each blew up a balloon and tied it. Then we squeezed our balloons, and they grew smaller. The air inside them took up less space. "Not only can gases be compressed," explained Dr. Gonzalez, "but they can expand to fill any size container." To test this, we popped our balloons with a pin. Dr. Gonzalez told us the pop was the sound of the air inside the balloon escaping through the hole and expanding to fill the room.

By this time, we were all ready for a snack. While preparing our snack, we investigated how heat affects the states of matter. We warmed chocolate sauce in the microwave. The warm chocolate was liquid. Then we each dipped an ice cream cone into the sauce. As the chocolate

When you pop a balloon, the air inside rushes out and expands to fill its new container.

WATER VAPOR

Water is the only substance on Earth that is commonly found in all three states. Only a tiny amount of the water on our planet is in the air as vapor. Most water on the planet is liquid or solid. When water vapor does form, it soon turns back into a liquid or a solid, falling as snow or rain. Water vapor is invisible. If you see fog, mist, or a cloud, the water is not vapor, but tiny water droplets. Each droplet is smaller than one-tenth the width of a human hair.

cooled, it hardened. Heating can change a solid into a liquid. It can also change a liquid into a gas.

We drank cups of ice water as we ate our ice cream cones. Dr. Gonzalez said we were experiencing water in all three states, and she asked if we could identify them. We knew we were drinking liquid water. We also figured out that ice is solid water. But where is the gas form of water? Dr. Gonzalez told us to hold our hands in front of our mouths and breathe on them. The breath made our hands moist. The moisture came from water vapor inside our lungs. ★

Dr. Gonzalez told us that today a scientist will come to talk to us about matter. But first, we had an experiment to do. We found a tub of water, a ball of clay, rocks, and a block of wood at our table. We spent the morning testing whether the objects were denser than water. This is easy to test because you just drop the objects in water and see if they sink or float.

We discovered that wood floats, but rocks sink. The ball of clay sinks, but you can make it float if you shape it into a little boat. We wondered why some things sink and some float.

Wood is less dense than water, so it floats. Even birds know wood is a great material for making boats.

THE MATTER OF DENSITY

As a substance changes from gas to liquid to solid, its density often changes. Usually the solid is heaviest, the gas is lightest, and the liquid is in the middle. But water is different. Solid water is less dense than liquid water. Ice floats. You know this because you have seen ice cubes float in a glass of water. When you skate on a frozen lake or pond, you can look through the ice and see liquid water trapped underneath.

Dr. Gonzalez told us that **density** is a measure of how heavy something is compared to its volume. Density has to do with how much matter is packed into a space. If the molecules are close together, the density is high. If the molecules are spread out, the density is low. Objects that are denser than water sink, and objects that are less dense than water float.

Next, Dr. Gonzalez showed us that an egg sinks in a tub of water. She tested another egg in a different tub of water, and this egg floated. Why did one egg float and the other egg sink? We were stumped. Then she told us the trick. The first tub contained freshwater. The egg is denser than freshwater, so it sinks. But the second tub was filled with saltwater. Saltwater is denser than freshwater and denser than the egg. So this time, the egg floats.

Fresh eggs sink in a bowl of freshwater. What might make these eggs float?

For our last experiment, we made liquid layers. We used four liquids: oil, corn syrup, water we dyed blue, and alcohol we dyed green. We poured the liquids one at a time into a glass jar. The corn syrup sank to the bottom of the jar. The blue water floated on top of the corn syrup. The oil floated on the water, and the green alcohol floated on top of everything else.

"Does anyone know why the liquids formed layers?" Dr. Gonzalez asked. Someone guessed that it had to do with differences in density. "Exactly right," said Dr. Gonzalez. "Each liquid has a different density. The denser liquids sank to the bottom, and the least dense liquids floated on top."

We learned that all kinds of matter can have different densities. A solid-gold brick is much heavier than a same-

Oil is less dense than water. When oil spills into oceans or lakes, it floats on the water's surface.

sized block of wood because gold is denser than wood. The layers in our experiment showed that liquids also have different densities. Even gases have different densities. Helium balloons float because the helium in the balloon is less dense than the surrounding air.

After exploring density on our own, we met Dr. Gabrielle Desmarais. She studies what happens when oil spills in the ocean. Because oil is less dense than water, the oil floats to the surface. She can make predictions about where the oil will spread in a spill. She uses a dye that has the same density as oil and will float like oil. By watching the dye, she can learn how oil spreads. She can predict where the spilled oil will go and how tides, winds, and ocean currents will spread the spill around. ★

Today we learned what happens when two kinds of matter are mixed together. That is called a mixture. Mixtures are all around us. A vegetable salad is a mixture of different vegetables. A chocolate chip cookie is a mixture of batter and chocolate chips. Soil is a mixture of sand, bits of rock, and the remains of living things. Metals can be mixtures. Brass is a mixture of copper and zinc. Even rocks can be mixtures.

Sometimes when two substances mix, one of them seems to disappear. Dr. Gonzalez showed us that if you stir salt into water, the tiny particles of salt vanish. The salt is

SEPARATING MIXTURES

How do you separate a mixture into its parts? Water from a lake is mixed with sand, dirt, and tiny living things. Filtering is one way to clean the water. The water passes through the filter, but the particles of dirt and sand get stuck. Another way to clean water is to heat it so the water becomes a gas. The gas goes into the air, and the dirt is left behind. The water vapor can then be captured in a clean container and cooled so it turns back into a liquid.

still there and you can taste it, but you can no longer see it. The salt has **dissolved**. This is a type of mixture called a **solution**.

We spent the morning investigating what sorts of things dissolve in water. Not everything makes a solution when you stir it into water. We found that sand, oil, rocks, and wax don't dissolve in water. But both baking soda and salt do dissolve, making a solution.

Dr. Sonya Nagi came to our classroom in the afternoon. She told us that liquids and solids aren't the only things that make solutions. Gases can also dissolve. She told us she studies how to make carbonated soft drinks. She is helping to develop soft drinks that are extra fizzy. The fizz comes from a gas called **carbon dioxide** that is dissolved in water.

Dr. Nagi showed us how to weigh the carbon dioxide in a bottle of orange soda. First we placed the bottle on an electronic balance, or scale, to weigh it. Then we shook the bottle for a few seconds and unscrewed the lid. The soda sprayed all over us. Dr. Nagi gave us some paper towels and a new bottle. She told us the trick is to open the cap very slowly to let out the gas without letting out any liquid.

We cleaned up and tried again. This time we shook the bottle and opened the cap slowly. Only the gas escaped,

Carbon dioxide gas makes soda fizzy. It can also make a mess!

and the liquid stayed inside. Then we recapped the bottle and weighed it. To our surprise, the bottle of orange soda weighed less. There was less carbon dioxide dissolved in the drink. With the cap tightly on, we shook the bottle again and opened it slowly. More gas came out. Every time we put it on the scale, the bottle of orange soda weighed less. We did this until we couldn't get any more carbon dioxide out of the drink. We calculated that the carbon dioxide in the orange soda weighed a little less than a penny. ★

Thursday: MATTER THAT BENDS, MATTER THAT BREAKS

What happens to solid matter when you try to bend it, squeeze it, or stretch it? Today we learned what happens when you try to **deform** solids. Some materials bend but stay in one piece when you fold or pull them. This is called **ductile** behavior.

Dr. Gonzalez scattered all sorts of objects around the room. She told us to try to find ones that were ductile. We found a stick of chewing gum, a ball of clay, and a sheet of aluminum foil. All these things bend without breaking. I discovered a pencil is not ductile. I tried to bend one and it snapped in half!

Next, Dr. Gonzalez explained that some materials are **brittle**. "When you try to deform something brittle, it breaks," she said. We were off on a hunt to find brittle objects. I had already discovered that a pencil is brittle. We added a candle, a clay flowerpot, and a glass jar to the list.

Finally, we learned about materials that are **elastic**. "If you bend or stretch something elastic and then let go," explained Dr. Gonzalez, "it returns to its original shape." Our list of elastic materials included a balloon, a rubber band, and a metal spring.

Then Dr. Gonzalez introduced us to Dr. Bill Barnes. He studies how rocks can be deformed. He told us that sometimes something ductile can be changed into something brittle, and vice versa. One way to do this is to change the temperature. If you freeze a stick of gum, it becomes brittle and snaps in two when you try to bend it. If you heat a candle, it becomes ductile and bends instead of breaking.

Dr. Barnes told us he studies the giant slabs of rock that make up Earth's outer shell. These slabs are called

Wet clay is ductile. You can mold it into any shape you like. If you bake it, it will keep that shape. Is baked clay ductile or brittle?

HEAT AND MATTER

Some matter carries heat well. You wouldn't want to walk barefoot across blacktop on a hot day. Blacktop absorbs heat. Not all matter absorbs heat easily, which is why it is comfortable to walk across a grassy lawn on a hot day. Engineers who design cars, airplanes, and spacecraft understand the importance of heat. They know which materials conduct heat and which don't. They use the right types of materials to keep the parts of the machine from getting too hot or too cold.

plates, and they cover the entire earth, fitting together like pieces of a jigsaw puzzle. The plates move around very slowly, sliding over a layer of molten rock. "Sometimes," Dr. Barnes said, "two plates collide or scrape against one another. What happens next depends on whether the rocks are brittle or ductile. If the rocks are brittle, they push together until one breaks." He explained that the result of brittle plates colliding is an earthquake. "But if the rocks are ductile, an earthquake won't happen. Instead, the rocks bend like clay and form a new shape. This is how some hills and mountains are formed."

Dr. Barnes told us he studies what makes a rock brittle or ductile. It depends on many factors, like what materials the rock is made of and how much water it contains. Another factor is temperature. Rocks near the earth's surface are cold, but rocks deep inside the earth are hot. Cold rocks tend to be brittle, and hot ones tend to be ductile. Another factor is how quickly the rocks push together. Quick movements tend to make rocks brittle. But if the rocks push together slowly, they are more likely to fold. ★

When these rocks pushed together, they folded to create new shapes. Were these rocks brittle or ductile when they collided?

Friday: MAKING NEW KINDS OF MATTER

Today we learned that some changes to matter are physical. This means the matter may have changed in some way, but it is still the same kind of matter. For example, when an ice cube melts, the matter hasn't changed into something new—it is still water. If you crumple a piece of aluminum foil, it is still aluminum, just in a different shape. If you break a rock, it is still a rock.

Some chemical reactions can be dangerous. Protective eyewear can help you stay safe. Always ask an adult before exploring chemical reactions on your own.

But sometimes matter changes into something new. This kind of change is called a chemical change. In a chemical change, the molecules of two substances meet and rearrange themselves into a new substance. This is called a chemical reaction.

We learned that chemical reactions go on all around us. Chemical reactions inside your stomach help you digest your food. Chemical reactions in a kitchen turn batter into cake. When wood burns in a fireplace, gasoline burns in a car engine, trees grow, or bread gets moldy, those are all chemical reactions.

An important thing to remember is that even though the old matter has disappeared and a new type of matter has replaced it, the amount of matter doesn't change. There is always the same amount of matter before and after a chemical reaction. The number of molecules hasn't changed. The molecules have just rearranged into something different.

Mr. Benjamin Brittain came to teach us more about chemical reactions. He explained that he studies rusting, a chemical reaction that happens to iron. "Iron is a useful material because it is easy to shape after being heated," Mr. Brittain told us. "Iron is used to make all kinds of things, like bridges, buildings, cars, and bicycles. But when iron interacts with oxygen in the air, it forms a new substance that is reddish brown and flaky. Most people call it rust. I call it iron oxide. Iron oxide is a problem because it is not strong like iron. Rusting can weaken anything made with iron." He also told us that iron rusts more quickly in moist air because water speeds up the chemical reaction.

To see rust in action, Mr. Brittain took us outside on a rust hunt. Once we started looking, we found rust everywhere. There was a rusty metal trash can and a rusty manhole cover in the street. We found a rusty old bicycle that looked like it had been left outside for a long time. We found rust on cars, especially where the paint was chipped away. We even found a birdhouse held together by nails that had rusted in the rain.

IRON IS EVERYWHERE

Iron is found on meteorites and on other planets. It is what gives the soil on Mars its red color. Scientists think the core of the earth may be made of hot, liquid iron. For more than one thousand years, people have been removing iron from the earth and using it to make tools. Living things even have iron inside of them. Plants draw iron out of the soil and use it for photosynthesis. You get iron from the food you eat. It helps your blood carry oxygen to your tissues.

Can you see where this bicycle is starting to rust? It needs a new coat of paint to help protect it.

Mr. Brittain told us he works with bicycle makers to develop special paints. These paints prevent bicycles from rusting. Rusting is not a big problem for kids who live in the desert because water speeds rusting, and the desert is dry most of the time. But if you live someplace where it rains or snows a lot and you leave your bicycle out, you can have a big problem. Paint protects the metal from the process of rusting. Painted metal does not come into contact with air. But if the paint is scratched, that spot can rust. So Mr. Brittain tries to develop paints that won't scratch easily. ★

Congratulations! You have explored the world of matter. You have learned about solids, liquids, and gases. You understand that matter can have different densities. You have seen that different things can happen when you mix two kinds of matter together. You have discovered the different ways matter behaves when it is deformed. Sometimes the matter bends, sometimes it breaks, and sometimes it bounces back. You have learned about chemical changes, when matter turns into a new kind of substance. Congratulations on a mission well done!

CONSIDER THIS

★ What happens to the air inside a balloon when you pop the balloon?

★ A teaspoon of sugar is stirred into one cup of water. A teaspoon of oil is stirred into another cup of water. What do you predict will happen in each case?

When an aircraft approaches the speed of sound, the air around it cools. Water vapor in the air returns to its liquid state and becomes a visible cone of water droplets.

★ In the liquid layers experiment, why did the liquids not mix together?

★ Two rocks collide and break. Two other rocks collide and fold. What is one factor that might have caused the difference?

★ Water, chocolate, and iron all change state when heated. What are some other materials that change from solid to liquid or from liquid to gas at different temperatures?

GLOSSARY

brittle (BRIH-tuhl) not flexible; easily broken

carbon dioxide (kahr-buhn dye-AHK-side) a gas formed from carbon and oxygen; carbon dioxide gas gives fizz to carbonated beverages

compress (kuhm-PRES) to squeeze matter into a smaller space

deform (di-FORM) to twist, pull, or squeeze out of shape

density (DEN-si-tee) how heavy or light a thing is for its size

dissolve (di-ZAHLV) to disappear into a liquid

ductile (DUHK-tuhl) can be stretched or folded without breaking

elastic (i-LAS-tik) able to return to its original shape after being deformed

mixture (MIKS-chur) a substance made of two or more gases, liquids, or solids

molecule (MAH-luh-kyool) the smallest particle of a material that has the same properties as that material

solution (suh-LOO-shuhn) a mixture of two substances where one is dissolved in the other

volume (VAHL-yoom) the amount of space occupied by a solid, liquid, or gas

LEARN MORE

BOOKS

Bailey, Jacqui. *The Rock Factory: The Story About the Rock Cycle.* Mankato, MN: Capstone, 2006.

Claybourne, Anna. *The Nature of Matter.* Pleasantville, NY: Gareth Stevens, 2007.

Green, Dan. *Physics: Why Matter Matters.* New York: Kingfisher, 2008.

Taylor, Charles. *The Kingfisher Science Encyclopedia.* New York: Kingfisher, 2006.

WEB SITES

Blue Planet

http://www.amnh.org/exhibitions/water/?section=blueplanet&page=blueplanet_d#

Learn about the science of water.

Edible/Inedible Experiments Archive

http://www.madsci.org/experiments

Try some fun experiments from the MadSci Network.

How Much CO2 is in a Bottle of Soda?

http://www.science-house.org/CO2/activities/co2/soda.html

Experiment to find how much carbon dioxide is in a bottle of soda.

WHAT A GAS

This experiment shows a chemical reaction in action. Do it in a sink or outdoors. Take an empty 1.5-liter plastic soda bottle and carefully fill it with 2 tablespoons of vinegar. Use a funnel to add 1 teaspoon of baking soda to the vinegar. Quickly slip a balloon over the neck of the bottle. You should see the balloon start to inflate. If nothing is happening, give the bottle a gentle shake. What is happening inside the bottle to cause the balloon to expand?

LIQUID LAYERS

Find a jar and make some liquid layers yourself! You can color each of the liquids with a drop of food coloring. Pour the liquids into the jar one at a time, starting with the densest. Here are some liquids to try, listed from densest to least dense: honey, corn syrup, dish soap, water, vegetable oil, baby oil, rubbing alcohol. What happens if you pour the liquids slowly? Do you get a different result if you pour the liquids quickly? What happens if you shake the jar after adding all the liquids? For more detailed instructions, see http://www.stevespanglerscience.com/experiment/seven-layer-density-column.

INDEX

ABOUT THE AUTHOR

Rebecca Hirsch holds a PhD in molecular biology from the University of Wisconsin–Madison. She worked as a scientist before becoming a writer. She writes for children and young adults on topics ranging from plants to polar bears. She lives with her husband and daughters in State College, Pennsylvania.

ABOUT THE CONSULTANTS

Heather Beck Abushanab has a PhD in Mechanical Engineering from MIT. She currently works as an adjunct professor at Wentworth Institute of Technology in Boston, MA, in the Applied Math and Sciences Department. Heather lives in Framingham, MA, with her husband and two children.

Gail Saunders-Smith is a former classroom teacher and Reading Recovery teacher leader. Currently she teaches literacy courses at Youngstown State University in Ohio. Gail is the author of many books for children and three professional books for teachers.